PLAYALONG ALTO SAX CHRISTMAS HITS

Published by
WISE PUBLICATIONS
14-15 Berners Street, London W1T 3LJ,
United Kingdom.

Exclusive Distributors:
MUSIC SALES LIMITED
Distribution Centre, Newmarket Road, Bury St Edmunds, Suffolk IP33 3YB,
United Kingdom.
MUSIC SALES PTY LIMITED
Units 3-4, 17 Willfox Street, Condell Park, NSW 2200, Australia.

Order No. AM1007237
ISBN 978-1-78305-242-4
This book © Copyright 2013 Wise Publications, a division of Music Sales Limited.

Unauthorised reproduction of any part of this publication by
any means including photocopying is an infringement of copyright.

Compiled and edited by Jenni Norey.
Cover designed by Michael Bell Design.
Printed in the EU.

Your Guarantee of Quality:
As publishers, we strive to produce every book to the highest commercial standards.
This book has been carefully designed to minimise awkward page turns and
to make playing from it a real pleasure.
Particular care has been given to specifying acid-free, neutral-sized paper made from
pulps which have not been elemental chlorine bleached.
This pulp is from farmed sustainable forests and was produced with special regard for the environment.
Throughout, the printing and binding have been planned to ensure a sturdy,
attractive publication which should give years of enjoyment.
If your copy fails to meet our high standards, please inform us and we will gladly replace it.

www.musicsales.com

31 MELODY LINE ARRANGEMENTS +
31 mp3 BACKING TRACKS +
31 mp3 DEMO TRACKS!

PLAYALONG ALTO SAX CHRISTMAS HITS

WISE PUBLICATIONS
part of The Music Sales Group
London / New York / Paris / Sydney / Copenhagen / Berlin / Madrid / Hong Kong / Tokyo

ALL I WANT FOR CHRISTMAS IS YOU MARIAH CAREY 9
(Carey/Afanasieff) Universal/MCA Music Limited/Sony/ATV Music Publishing (UK) Limited

BABY, IT'S COLD OUTSIDE DEAN MARTIN 12
(Loesser) MPL Communications Limited

BLUE CHRISTMAS ELVIS PRESLEY 14
(Hayes/Johnson) Moncur Street Music Ltd

C-H-R-I-S-T-M-A-S PERRY COMO 16
(Carson/Arnold) Carlin Music Corporation

THE CHRISTMAS SONG (CHESTNUTS ROASTING ON AN OPEN FIRE) MEL TORME 18
(Torme/Wells) Chappell/Morris Limited

THE CHRISTMAS WALTZ FRANK SINATRA 20
(Cahn/Styne) Westminster Music Limited/Imagem Music

FAIRYTALE OF NEW YORK THE POGUES 22
(MacGowan/Finer) Universal Music Publishing Limited/Universal Music Publishing MGB Limited

HAPPY XMAS (WAR IS OVER) JOHN LENNON 24
(Lennon/Ono) Lenono Music

HARK! THE HERALD ANGELS SING TRADITIONAL 26
(Wesley/Mendelssohn) Dorsey Brothers Music Limited

HAVE YOURSELF A MERRY LITTLE CHRISTMAS FRANK SINATRA 28
(Martin/Blane) EMI United Partnership Limited

HERE COMES SANTA CLAUS GENE AUTRY 34
(Autry/Haldeman) Campbell Connelly & Company Limited

HOME FOR THE HOLIDAYS PERRY COMO 30
(Stillman/Allen) Campbell Connelly & Company Limited/Edward Kassner Music Company

I BELIEVE IN FATHER CHRISTMAS GREG LAKE 37
(Lake/Sinfield) Leadchoice Limited

I SAW MOMMY KISSING SANTA CLAUS TOMMIE CONNER 40
(Connor) Blue Ribbon Music Limited

I WISH IT COULD BE CHRISTMAS EVERY DAY WIZARD 46
(Wood) EMI Music Publishing Limited

IN DULCI JUBILO TRADITIONAL 43
(Traditional) Dorsey Brothers Music Limited

JINGLE BELL ROCK CHUBBY CHECKER 50
(Beal/Boothe) TRO Essex Music Limited

JINGLE BELLS TRADITIONAL 48
(Pierpont) Dorsey Brothers Music Limited

LET IT SNOW! LET IT SNOW! LET IT SNOW! DORIS DAY 54
(Cahn/Styne) Imagem Music/Warner/Chappell North America Limited

LONELY THIS CHRISTMAS MUD 56
(Chinn/Chapman) Universal Music Publishing MGB Limited

MERRY XMAS EVERYBODY SLADE 51
(Holder/Lea) Barn Publishing (Slade) Limited

MISTLETOE AND WINE CLIFF RICHARD 58
(Stewart/Paul/Strachan) Patch Music Limited

PEACE ON EARTH/LITTLE DRUMMER BOY DAVID BOWIE 64
(Kohan/Grossman/Fraser) Chelsea Music Publishing Co. Limited/Phraser-Morton Music/Warner/Chappell North America Limited

SANTA BABY EARTHA KITT 66
(Javits/Springer/Springer) TM Music Limited

SILENT NIGHT TRADITIONAL 72
(Mohr/Gruber) Dorsey Brothers Music Limited

SLEIGH RIDE LEROY ANDERSON 69
(Parish/Anderson) EMI Music Publishing Limited

A SPACEMAN CAME TRAVELLING CHRIS DE BURGH 6
(de Burgh) Chrysalis Music Limited

STOP THE CAVALRY JONA LEWIE 74
(Lewie) Imagem London

WALKING IN THE AIR ALED JONES 76
(Blake) Chester Music Limited

WINTER WONDERLAND PERRY COMO 78
(Smith/Bernard) Redwood Music Limited/Francis Day & Hunter Limited

WONDERFUL CHRISTMASTIME PAUL McCARTNEY 61
(McCartney) MPL Communications Limited

SEE PAGE 80 FOR DETAILS OF HOW TO ACCESS YOUR TRACKS

A Spaceman Came Travelling

Words & Music by Chris de Burgh

All I Want For Christmas Is You

Words & Music by Mariah Carey & Walter Afanasieff

Baby, It's Cold Outside

Words & Music by Frank Loesser

Blue Christmas

Words & Music by Billy Hayes & Jay Johnson

C-H-R-I-S-T-M-A-S

Words by Jenny Lou Carson
Music by Eddy Arnold

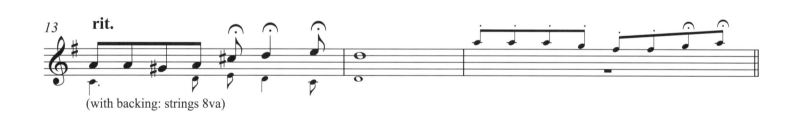

© Copyright 1949 Hill & Range Songs Incorporated, USA.
Carlin Music Corporation.
All Rights Reserved. International Copyright Secured.

The Christmas Song (Chestnuts Roasting On An Open Fire)

Words & Music by Mel Torme & Robert Wells

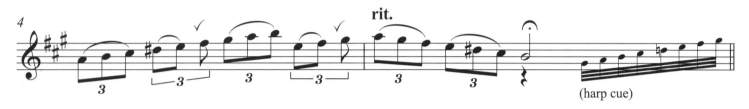

© Copyright 1946 (Renewed) Edwin H. Morris & Company Incorporated, USA.
Chappell/Morris Limited.
All Rights Reserved. International Copyright Secured.

The Christmas Waltz

Words by Sammy Cahn
Music by Jule Styne

Fairytale Of New York

Words & Music by Shane MacGowan & Jem Finer

Happy Xmas (War Is Over)

Words & Music by John Lennon & Yoko Ono

Hark! The Herald Angels Sing

Words by Charles Wesley
Music by Felix Mendelssohn

Have Yourself A Merry Little Christmas

Words & Music by Hugh Martin & Ralph Blane

© Copyright 1944 EMI Feist Catalog Incorporated.
EMI United Partnership Limited.
All Rights Reserved. International Copyright Secured.

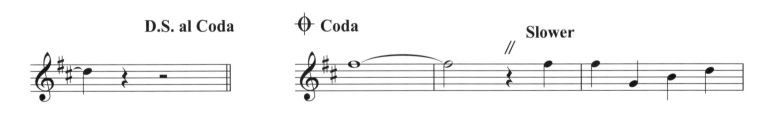

(There's No Place Like) Home For The Holidays

Words & Music by Al Stillman & Robert Allen

Here Comes Santa Claus
(Right Down Santa Claus Lane)

Words & Music by Gene Autry & Oakley Haldeman

I Believe In Father Christmas

Words & Music by Greg Lake & Peter Sinfield

© Copyright 1975 Leadchoice Limited.
Excerpt from "Lieutenant Kije" by Sergei Prokofiev included by permission of the copyright owners, Boosey & Hawkes Music Publishers Limited.
All Rights Reserved. International Copyright Secured.

I Saw Mommy Kissing Santa Claus

Words & Music by Tommie Connor

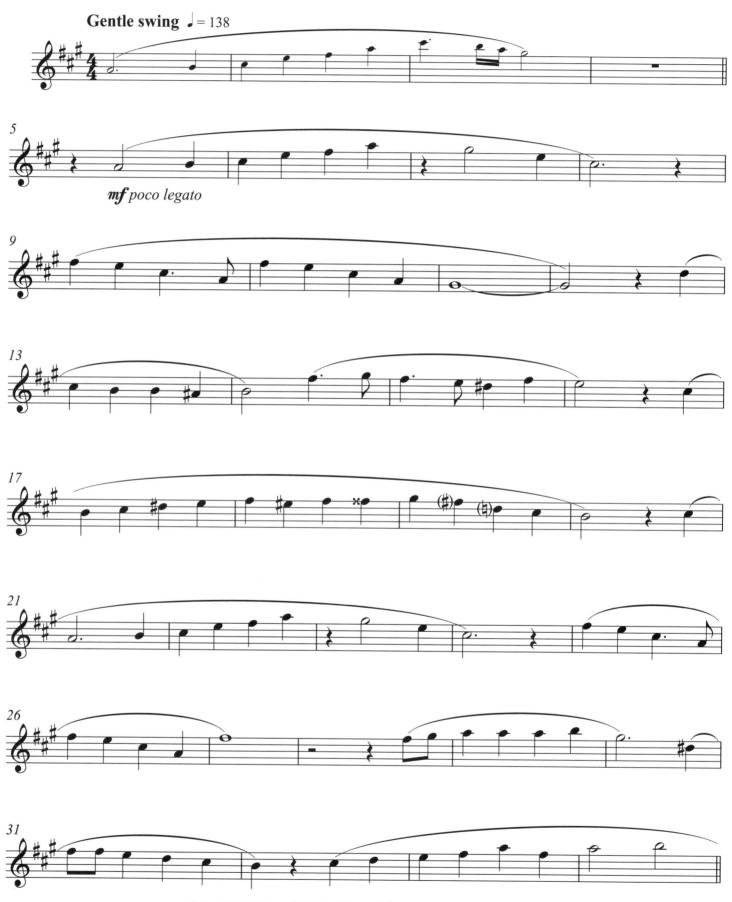

In Dulci Jubilo

Words & Music Traditional

Brightly, with a bounce ♩. = 120

© Copyright 2010 Dorsey Brothers Music Limited.
All Rights Reserved. International Copyright Secured.

(guitar solo)

I Wish It Could Be Christmas Every Day

Words & Music by Roy Wood

Jingle Bells

Words & Music by James Lord Pierpont

© Copyright 2010 Dorsey Brothers Music Limited.
All Rights Reserved. International Copyright Secured.

Jingle Bell Rock

Words & Music by Joseph Beal & James Boothe

Merry Xmas Everybody

Words & Music by Neville Holder & James Lea

Let It Snow! Let It Snow! Let It Snow!

Words by Sammy Cahn
Music by Jule Styne

Lonely This Christmas

Words & Music by Nicky Chinn & Mike Chapman

Mistletoe And Wine

Words by Leslie Stewart & Jeremy Paul
Music by Keith Strachan

Wonderful Christmastime

Words & Music by Paul McCartney

© Copyright 1979 MPL Communications Limited.
All Rights Reserved. International Copyright Secured.

Peace On Earth/Little Drummer Boy

Words by Alan Kohan
Music by Larry Grossman & Ian Fraser

© Copyright 1977 One Zee Music Administered by Chelsea Music Publishing Co. Ltd/
Phraser-Morton Music/Warner/Chappell North America Limited.
All Rights Reserved. International Copyright Secured.

Santa Baby

Words & Music by Joan Javits, Phil Springer & Tony Springer

Sleigh Ride

Words by Mitchell Parish
Music by Leroy Anderson

Silent Night

Words by Joseph Mohr
Music by Franz Gruber

Stop The Cavalry

Words & Music by Jona Lewie

Walking In The Air
(Theme from 'The Snowman')

Words & Music by Howard Blake

© Copyright 1982 Highbridge Music Limited.
All rights assigned in 2010 to Chester Music Limited.
© Copyright 2010 Chester Music Limited.
All Rights Reserved. International Copyright Secured.

Winter Wonderland

Words by Richard Smith
Music by Felix Bernard

© Copyright 1934 Francis Day & Hunter Limited.
All Rights Reserved. International Copyright Secured.

HOW TO DOWNLOAD YOUR MUSIC TRACKS

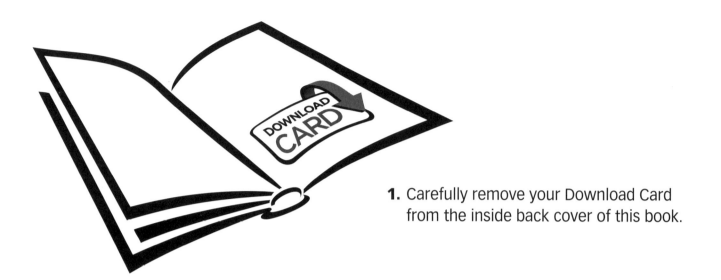

1. Carefully remove your Download Card from the inside back cover of this book.

2. On the back of the card is your unique access code. Enter this at www.musicsalesdownloads.com

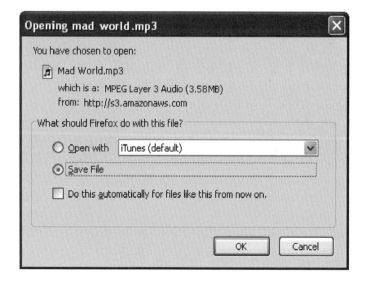

3. Follow the instructions to save your files to your computer*. That's it!

*Appearance of download manager will vary depending upon operating system and web browser.
In case of difficulty when downloading files, please contact dropcards.com/help
Card missing? Please contact music@musicsales.co.uk